FREE
your
SPIRIT

Other Books by Victoria Reynolds

Transcending Fear

Own Your True Worth

Rise Up

FREE
your
SPIRIT

5 Steps to Becoming Fearless
and Trusting Your Own Path

VICTORIA REYNOLDS

Free Your Spirit: 5 Steps to Becoming Fearless and Trusting Your Own Path

Copyright © 2020 by Victoria Reynolds

Published by FREESTYLE PRESS
Hermosa Beach, CA 90277

Because of the dynamic nature of the Internet, any web addresses or links contained in this book may have changed since publication and may no longer be valid.

Printed in the United States

ISBN: 978-1-954250-00-0 (sc)
ISBN: 978-1-954250-01-7 (ebk)

Cover Design by Chelsey Marie Clark
Cover Photo by Kenda Kerscher
Editing provided by Writing Goddess, Teri Breier

Freestyle Press

This guidebook is for every person who has the courage to leave the trodden path in search of higher ground.

"Is it possible that there is something we don't fully understand about God, and the understanding of which could change everything?"

— NEALE DONALD WALSCH

TABLE OF CONTENTS

"Being fearless isn't about not feeling fear. Fearlessness is recognizing fear and choosing to rise above it."

INTRODUCTION

As a little girl I was taught, "life is that men might have joy," and I took it to mean that joy didn't apply to women. It seemed to me that women were meant for suffering in service to men. In my religious indoctrination, I picked up that suffering made a woman appear more beautiful in the eyes of God and the men she served, and suffering in silence was evidence of her devoted submission to God's will. That belief continually seeped into my mind and my sense of worthiness as I watched the women around me sacrifice themselves to meet the needs and desires of everyone else, in what I now recognize as servitude.

Such was the case within the extremely patriarchal and very puritanical belief system of my childhood. It took many years for me to understand that "man" in our ancient texts was intended to be inclusive of all humankind. "Man" really meant "all."

Men wrote for other men and women were primarily excluded from most of the human story since the beginning of recorded time, but not necessarily from the true overall meaning. Women needed to go through men for guidance, even if the guidance was misgiven.

Inspiration has needed to go through the layers of men's egoic minds in our his-story, and as a result, we only have the male side of the story, along with masculine beliefs, perceptions and personal interpretations to reflect upon and learn from. That is part of our collective patriarchy. This is neither good nor bad, it simply is that it is and was what it was. Now, of course, we know that inspiration isn't limited to the minds of men.

According to many belief systems, life is that we might have joy. But how many people are really living a happy and genuinely joy-filled life? Instead, many are living lives of suffering and quiet desperation, and some not so quietly. We see them on the news, creating chaos in their lives and in the lives of others. Some go to the extreme of terrorizing others in attempt to release their own internal suffering.

If life is that we might have joy, why do so many people feel sad and miserable?

This question and inner awareness came to me during my mid-life transition, what I sometimes call my personal Holy Shift, and subsequent excavation. This inner exploration led me toward what became a truly fulfilling physical, mental, emotional, and spiritual transformation as I came to see what is true for me.

The breakthrough into my authentic self stemmed from desperation, after many years of feeling not quite right. There had always been an elusive void, a feeling that something was missing, that I could not figure out how to fill. Not that I was unhappy, just unfulfilled. Then I was hit by the mid-life turmoil that sucked me into a downward spiral of despair and, in the process, brought me home to me.

Perhaps for you, just as it was with me,

life may feel somewhat less like desperation and more as though something is missing. Something that you can't quite put your finger on and really clarify. Maybe it's a subtle feeling of emptiness that no amount of money or gain can seem to fill. Perhaps it is just a nagging feeling, lurking in the deepest recesses of your subconscious. Possibly there are unconscious feelings, thoughts, and beliefs that are running the show, affecting all your relationships and experiences, and making it difficult to fully trust life.

No matter how hard you try, regardless of how successful or unsuccessful you might be, does it seem like something is missing? Do you sometimes find yourself justifying what you have or feeling guilty for your success? Maybe there is a slight sense of shame for wanting more from your life? Perhaps it's not all that obvious. It may be so subtle that you don't even recognize what the nagging feeling is—you just know you aren't feeling as happy as it seems you should be.

The reason there are so many unhappy and unfulfilled people in this world is not because they don't have money, or love, or anything that supposedly creates happiness. Some of the wealthiest people in the world, even those who have everything society tells us "should" make them happy, are living empty lives. In contrast, there are some people who appear to have nothing of real value, yet they somehow live lives of contentment. Why is that? It all comes down to one simple thing – spiritual freedom.

Even if they don't know what to call it, those who are genuinely happy are following a path that feels right and in alignment with their own inner loving truth, whatever that truth is. Not what they think is right, based on external expectations or what they've been told to believe, but what feels good, right, and best for them, on a deep intrinsic level.

They have a richly profound connection to their own guidance system; an inner voice that directs and leads them with an inherent sense of being and moving through life. They aren't emotionally attached to their physical belongings. As much as humanly possible, they remain detached from the many beliefs and expectations inflicted on them throughout life, while continually searching for and releasing beliefs that no longer resonate with who they see themselves becoming. They seem to deeply and fundamentally be at peace with themselves, the people moving through life around them, and circumstances that arrive in their personal field. This peace has nothing to do with being attached to a system of belief and everything to do with being able to view their lives through a clear, unobstructed lens.

Many people consciously, and often unconsciously, cling to beliefs that block them from their highest and greatest good. These beliefs act like roadblocks on their paths, preventing them from understanding their truly infinite potential as individuals, and as a species.

Every fully functional human being is innately brilliant beyond measure, capable of creating a beautifully rewarding and richly meaningful life. Potential for greatness is encoded into all beings and is only limited by belief. Where a person came from, how they were raised, and their level of education, has been proven time and again to be inconsequential to happiness. You have probably heard numerous stories about people who overcame unsurmountable odds to find greatness within themselves. Their greatness was always there, it just needed to be cultivated by belief. Greatness, of course, isn't about fame and fortune—it's about having a bigger purpose in life and trusting it.

How do we measure the capacity for greatness? Certainly not through traditional methods. Using only an educational I.Q. to determine individual capacity for greatness is akin to using a thermometer to determine one's height. We need measuring tools that assess the many forms of intelligence; or better yet, let's throw out measurement and judgement entirely to allow everyone to be at peace with their own unique giftedness and limitless potential.

Greatness is grown and nurtured. It is cultivated through resilience and a willingness to follow a loving path that others may fear to tread. By trusting our own path, we create peace and heaven within ourselves, even when it doesn't look that way to others. Heaven on earth and peace on the planet begins with creating it within ourselves as individuals.

The peace on earth many of us say we want begins first with making personal peace with ourselves: including all of who we once were and have become. It is making peace with even our most painful stories, circumstances, situations, and relationships, along with the beliefs surrounding them. It also means making peace with our collective past and

12

present human story. All of that is the result of spiritual freedom; learning to see everything in our world from a new, loving perspective.

The purpose of this book is to help you uncover the source of beliefs that may be blocking you from achieving the life of joy and fulfillment that is your divine birthright. In the pages that follow, I offer insights to help you move forward in the quest to free your spirit and to help you find the courage to follow and trust your own unique path.

This guide is intended to help you begin the process of seeing your beliefs from a new perspective and hopefully cause you to consider more deeply about who you are and who you want to become.

All my teachings and insights are based on what I refer to as "practical spirituality."

One thing I've discovered over the years is that spirituality, when taken too seriously, can become just as dogmatic as organized religion; in essence, becoming just like any other religion where someone else is held on a pedestal at the top, rather than trusting the loving truth within. It becomes just another box of beliefs to transcend on the path toward a direct connection to Spirit.

Practical spirituality is found in your own connection to "Self" and your own truth, rather than following the beliefs of anyone or anything else. It is your connection to your own soul and what it knows is true and best for your personal evolution. It is the grounding cord of your connection to spirit, whatever that means to you.

Much of what I teach is based on the

concept that fear is the opposite of love. (I have discovered that fear is actually the lowest vibration of love, but I will save that for another time, since it is an advanced concept that took me a long time to grasp.)

Fear, in its many forms and functions, is the primary reason humanity is where it currently is. Individually and collectively, we are all affected, every moment of every day, by fear. We live in a reality based in fear and our challenge is to learn how to liberate ourselves from its control and follow love's guidance. Once we free our minds and hearts from the influence of fear, everything becomes possible.

In my book, *Transcending Fear*, I go into greater detail as I share my own personal journey of freedom and the principles that my inner therapist gave me to heal my life. I used these principles, what I have since come to call the *Transcendence Process,* to remedy my past and work through many of the fear-based beliefs that were implanted in my young mind during childhood. I still use them daily to keep me on a peaceful path. In that book, I also openly share the process I used to overwrite my fear-based beliefs with my own inner truths, to help readers process their own beliefs and past pain stories.

You can purchase a copy of *Transcending Fear* on my website at VictoriaReynolds.com and online wherever books are sold.

In this book, I share some of my story, along with inspiration to guide you on your personal path and journey to higher ground.

One last note before diving into the teaching in the pages of this book. You will come across words that may appear to be incorrectly capitalized. These are not editing errors but rather an intentional way of expressing big ideas. For example, when speaking of love as the essence of God, Love will be capitalized to differentiate it from emotions of love. This will also be the case for many of the other names for God, which for me is energy rather than an anthropomorphic male.

"Liberate yourself from the confines of fear-based beliefs and there you will find the courage to move with grace."

STEP 1:

Understand Spiritual Freedom

When I was a teenager, after experiencing too many traumas, I found myself in a battle, or perhaps an affair, with committing suicide. The visions of freeing myself from my personal hell consumed me for several years until I finally felt driven to decide between which hell seemed least painful. In my world, I was given three choices, all of which dammed me to an eternity in what I imagined as infinite hell. Our names and descriptions for hell differed from other religions, but all led to permanent banishment of the soul.

There was no way I could possibly win at the game of life – of that I was certain. I was a teenage girl from a cult where girls were only valued for clean, virginal wombs. And, since my virginity had been stolen from me, I had no real value. I could choose to stay in the community, living a life of personal hell, inevitably marrying a man I didn't love, sharing him with a bunch of other women I didn't like, and trust it was a guarantee to be allowed into the right level someday in our hierarchal, multi-level heaven. There, I would spend eternity having his babies so that he could be a God of his own planet. He would be a God and I would be one of his many consorts. That may have been a man's idea of heaven, but it didn't interest me, not in the least.

Second choice? Committing suicide and getting an immediate pass to an eternity in hell. That was truly tempting, and I almost jumped on it. I was so very, very tired of living and nothing about my suffering felt beautiful or rewarding. I needed out of my life! My final option – running away from home and leaving behind my religion – would deem me an apostate and guarantee another spot in God's eternal prison.

In my desperate mind, all choices led to a lifetime and eternity in hell; so the choice was dying and going to hell immediately or dragging life out and taking my chances of going to hell later. I only knew I could not stay in the life I was in. I simply could not continue to face the insult to my soul and maintain a facade of happiness. In one moment of clarity, just as I was about to end my life, my inner voice came to my rescue. "What if everything they've ever told you is a lie?" it whispered. That was enough for me to save my own life.

I chose to leave everything I knew behind to search for my happiness in a world that I had been taught my entire life to fear, while risking that everything I had been taught throughout my childhood was a deception. By a twist of fate, I found my way to freedom and discovered a whole new path to follow.

It was not only the first choice I had ever made for myself, but the best choice of my life. I chose to leave the path my parents and religion insisted was God's plan; the predestined path for me, created by Him for only the chosen few. As one of His favorite pre-birth daughters, God had chosen me for a destiny in polygamy. But that never felt quite right for me and my spirit yearned to be free.

Leaving home, I escaped my hypothetical destiny as a plural wife and found instead the path that was the true and right one for me. I found freedom, first for my body, then my mind, followed by my heart, and eventually my soul. My soul, my all of me, became free after years of letting go of what wasn't really me. And I found purpose, my true purpose – one that I could have never even imagined as a child.

What I found was spiritual freedom, freedom from fear-based beliefs and courage to trust my own path, rather than the "shoulds" others attempted to place on me. That freedom of spirit is what I share with you.

It is important to begin this guidebook with understanding what spiritual freedom is, and what it is not. Spiritual freedom is not the same as freedom of religion. Many religions are fear-based, even unknowingly; that is how subtle fear can be. Spiritual freedom is closer to freedom *from* religion because spiritual freedom is freedom from fear.

For myself, freeing my mind, body, heart, and spirit from religion is one of the best things I've ever done. It freed me to be true to myself, really trust who I am here to be, and fully trust my connection to higher guidance. It removed the middleman and provided me with a direct connection to Spirit. This may not be the case for you, as some people seem to need a master, but it has been true for me.

It began with the process of first freeing myself physically as a teenager, following a battle with suicidal thoughts and trying to be who my religion wanted me to be, then continued emotionally and mentally in my 20s as I discovered self-help books. Spiritually, my freedom occurred as the result of my mid-life transition, what I came to see as my personal awakening. At a time when my life was falling apart, a fearful voice in my head said, "what if they were right?" I was stunned that the thought was anywhere inside me. Until that time, I had forgotten spirituality of any kind, entirely. That one question was enough to start me on a new spiritual path of finding what was true and right for me. As a result, I came to connect with my higher self and inner loving truth.

Overall, my spiritual freedom occurred as the result of a mid-life crisis, which I am now so incredibly grateful for. It led to the discovery that many of the limiting beliefs resulting from my childhood religion (because everything in my childhood revolved around religion) were still dictating my life on a subconscious level, and blocking the happiness that I now recognize is every human being's birthright.

Spiritual freedom was the result of freeing my spirit, my vibrancy, from the constraints of fear that once held it captive. As I freed my spirit from the fearful beliefs still encapsulating my heart, life became so much more rewarding, in so many ways, than I had ever even thought possible. This freedom gave me a rich, profound connection to Spirit that my religion would have never allowed.

To clarify, *my* freedom came as the result of liberating myself from the fear-based beliefs that were a part of my life experience, stemming from childhood religion. This, of course, is not the case for everyone. Because my religion was the only thing I knew as a child, it was also my primary delivery source of fear. For others, the fear-based indoctrination may have originated from someplace else. Such conditioning can come from even the most well-meaning parents, teachers, and caregivers. It permeates television, media, and entertainment. It is continually being fed to us from everywhere outside of us, until we are mature enough to make the distinction and rise above it into love. That love-based realty is where our spirit is free.

Spirit is energy. It is the part of each of us that is connected to all that is.

Your soul is unable to achieve its greatest potential through you, assisting you in fulfilling all that you are fully capable of, while you are still held captive by fear in its many forms. It cannot manifest your greatness hiding under a bushel of fear and limitations that control your mind, heart, and body. You are the holder and beholder of your spirit, the limitless energy of which moves you through life and guides your path. It is what helps you know when you are off-track and resonates when you are spot-on.

All disease ("dis-ease") is the result of being out of ease, stemming from misalignment and lack of congruence with what is best for you. It is often your body's way of getting your attention as it attempts to bring you back to wholeness and onto the right path.

The whole of you; your mind, body, heart, and spirit, work together at their best performance when you are at ease. Ease is our natural state of being. This ease is freedom of the spirit as it guides you to reach for your fullest potential with grace rather than strife.

The human spirit, the light that exists

within every one of us, yearns to be free from the layers of fear that far too often hold it captive. Our spirit yearns to express itself without limits, through us. It is light-hearted, wild, expressive, adventurous, kind, brilliant, inspired, radiant, and filled with laughter. It sees the expansive beauty and wonder in all things. It wants to create without limits and explore boundless horizons. It wants to spread its proverbial wings and touch the world with our gifts. It wants to spread love like starlight and enlighten everything it touches.

The human spirit exists to experience all that it means to be fully alive, to learn, feel, grow, expand, and evolve. And yet, far too many of our pervasive beliefs attempt to contain it and restrict how we can access and experience it. Society's systems want to lock our limitless energy into boxes and label us.

Regardless of how pretty the box may be packaged, it is still a box; and many of us can no longer be contained.

Many of us, even perhaps unknowingly, now find ourselves searching for more, looking for greater possibilities for our soul's personal experience and higher understanding of spirit. We want to stand outside the box and see what lies beyond the realm of age-old thinking.

We want to feel the ease and freedom of exploring new understandings and experiences without the numerous constraints of packaged systems or their archaic practices. We are tired of believing what no longer resonates within our expansive soul. Many of us can no longer limit our own minds to the beliefs and practices that have been manipulated by the minds of many men over countless centuries.

For us, the beliefs and practices of our ancestors have served their purpose and no longer meet our personal spiritual needs. We have simply outgrown them as we search for higher and deeper understanding of the human experience, compelled by the insight that there is more out there for us to know.

Spiritual freedom is the peaceful result of remembering who you were at the time of your birth and re-becoming who you were always meant to be: that one, beautiful, magnificent you that no one else can be. It is being free to be yourself, whom you know deep inside yourself to be. It is being free to follow the guidance of the truth that calls to you from the core of your being. It is the freedom to be your *true* self, wholly, completely, and deliberately. It means living courageously, unrestricted by the many expectations, perceptions, beliefs, judgements, condemnations, and contradictions of anyone. It is being free from all those fears within yourself, as well.

This requires a continual process of growth and introspection, self-awareness and personal evolution. It means learning to love your whole-self, all of you, as you begin letting go of any judgements you may hold against yourself and accept the parts of you that have been rejected. It is being free of the seemingly endless depths of self-sabotaging, belittling, limiting, and restricting beliefs, conjured in fear by your mind and the minds of others.

It is having the courage to be in complete ownership of your own unique path and loving purpose. It is processing all your painful stories and transmuting them with love. It is taking full responsibility of your past and present beliefs, perceptions, and actions so you can consciously create your present and future reality.

It is internalizing – in every thought, belief, action, feeling, perception, and experience – the truth that you are intrinsically worthy of everything you desire; simply because you exist.

Spiritual freedom is the freedom to live your daily life, free of fear-based perspectives. It creates fearlessness as you come to recognize fear in its many appearances. It is understanding that fear exists simply as a medium for growth and allows you to forgive those who use it as a tool for control. It means seeing which of your internal beliefs require your personal attention and inspection, in order to work through them. Spiritual freedom is seeing all of life, and everyone in it, through love and understanding.

It is seeing all that exists through the

infinite loving eyes of what many call God – the eyes of unconditional love.

The One Universal Mind, Divine Allness, the Great Master-Mind, the ever-present, all-knowing, infinite-intelligence, infinite-wisdom, all-loving, all-giving, infinite-power, infinite-love, the Heavenly Father and/or Mother, Creator, Source Energy, Allah, Yahweh (AKA God, by whatever name or label you give It) sees all of life and all of Its creations as perfection, with absolute love for all that is. It is the energy of Love itself.

Anything less than love is ego aligned with fear, and is a uniquely human perspective.

Spiritual freedom is every person's experience with their own spirituality, even when they don't see themselves as being particularly spiritual.

Many people, from an absence of awareness otherwise, confuse religion with spirituality. Spiritualty and religion are two vastly different experiences which are often sandwiched together for delivery to the masses. Spiritualty exists perfectly well on its own without the constraints of systems to hold, confine, and deliver it. However, throughout our known human story, the practices of religion and spiritualty have been so deeply intertwined that many people simply cannot see or recognize the difference between them, and are unable to experience them separately.

Religiosities, the vast and diverse systems of belief, can and do often create the illusion of separation and disconnection. All religions hold varying degrees of loving spirituality within their core, yet many religions create a barrier to fully accessing Spirit. They often feed fear and belief in separation from God as they set themselves up as a middleman of sorts.

Religions are the dogma, the rules by which a given belief system claims is the path to God, much of which is often based in fear disguised as love.

In my own perspective, all religions are publicly-labeled and human-enabled delivery systems. Each one of us has the freedom to choose which delivery system to use, if any at all. Delivery systems become unnecessary when you understand that spirituality is a uniquely personal experience and that it is always, immediately, and directly accessible to anyone who knows to look for it.

Spirituality is limitless and is the all-loving, always available connection to Spirit; ourselves, the divine nature of our being, and to the infinite universal intelligence and womb of creation many call God.

This connection to Spirit exists perfectly well, and is often easier to access, outside the many confines of religious dogma. One need not follow a specific master or go through any given middleman to get to God. Spirituality, without the religious constraints, has limitless freedom to be all that it has the ability to be through us.

In spiritual freedom we have the ability to self-regulate through love, rather than being controlled by fear. A free spirit finds love within oneself. The heart is where love resides and is the heaven we all seek to find. We never really left it and were never separate from it. We just needed to find our way home within ourselves.

Each of us is born whole, complete, and perfect (although it might not always look that way) as boundless beings of love. In our present, fear-based reality, we then learn fear as a protective way of maneuvering through our many life experiences. We create fear-based beliefs as a form of self-preservation, which, exploited, then become societal controls. These fearful beliefs are often based on the perceptions and expectations of those around us as we grow and are a part of the culture we are subjected to.

In attempting to live our lives by the many expectations and beliefs of others, and even by what they say God expects of us, we begin to lose ourselves in the process. As we confine our limitless spirits to the labels and perceptions of those around us, we lose much of our inner loving essence and our own direct connection to the Infinite.

While this inner connection is never

completely severed, our stream of consciousness, the light that exists within every one of us, can become so thin and dimmed that many people can no longer recognize it in themselves or in others. For some, their inner light becomes so dimmed that all they know is fear, pain, and suffering. As a result, they feel the only way to ease their own pain is to cause the suffering and pain of others. They can no longer hear, see, or feel the loving presence that came with them at the time of birth and they become lost in the storm of fear. Some fall for the false belief that they can find happiness through greed, control, and manipulation of others, which really only leads to further depletion of their heart's light.

Because they have lost their inner connection, they lose their way in the darkness. They conclude that someone else must be to blame who is responsible for their suffering.

They simply cannot see that the path back to Love, to a life of peace and joy, is accessible through themselves.

As fear continues to take more control of their minds and encapsulate their hearts, they blindly follow the way everyone else around them is following, because they are told it is the only way. They search for peace, love, and light outside of themselves because that is where they have been told to look for it.

Blindly following the way that had been supposedly laid before them, they stop listening to their own inner guidance in the need and desire for acceptance from others. Blind faith often leads to spiritual blindness and take can one down a very dark and painful path.

For many human beings, their once limitless spirit becomes locked away until they have an awakening, a moment or series of experiences that causes them to open their eyes and stop playing along with the charade. They begin to see how they've been played, and start to listen to the voice within them that knows who they are and the path their soul wants them to take. They begin to see, feel, and experience that beautiful, unique path and purpose that is solely and soully (misspelling intended) theirs to follow. They begin to find their way back home to love, peace, and heaven within.

It bears repeating that spiritual freedom is the ultimate freedom. It is liberating yourself from the confines of fear-based beliefs. It is freedom from the boxes and labels that have been placed upon you. It is being free to be authentically and innately who you are and not who anyone else expects you to be. It is the freedom to live in your own truth. It is the freedom to trust the path that you, your own soul's infinite wisdom, created and continues to create for you.

On your own individual, unique path, your spirit is free to soar, and here you begin to experience the fullness of your freedom of spirit.

With a spirit that is free from the constraints of fear, all things become available.

"Know your truth
and the truth will set
you free."

STEP 2:

KNOW THE TRUTH ABOUT TRUTH

I grew up with a completely irrational belief (as I now see it) that there is only one true church, one true prophet, and one right way to God. That there was only one path and that if I fell off that one very straight and narrow path, my soul would be lost to an eternity of darkness.

To never question this idea that there was only one path and one truth left me in a world of pain and self-loathing for my imperfection and constant fear of the judgmental and narcissistic heavenly father of my childhood religion.

Many, like me, are taught that truth is truth and that there is only one-right-way...that God is infallible and never changes...that all truths are unwavering, universal, immutable, and absolute.

Yes, there are universal truths and those truths are undisputable. Without unwavering constants provided through universal laws, there would be chaos. Those truths are often referred to as the *Immutable Laws of the Universe*, and many have been studied by science to be more than just quantum theory or spiritual speculation.

Personal truths are just that, personal. As I mentioned in the last chapter, Spirit is energy.

Because I see them as the same, I am inclined to use both words interchangeably. For example, a highly-spirited horse doesn't mean the horse goes to church. Get the picture?

Science, in my mind, has a much better grasp on Spirit than religion. That is, until religion evolves to more greatly incorporate scientific understanding; as it always inevitably does, however begrudgingly, when the evidence becomes indisputable.

As more and more people search for higher understanding of Spirit, and a deeper, more personal understanding of truth, many are now leaving behind organized religion. As we evolve to become more loving and raise our consciousness, we will no longer want fear-based constraints to limit us. It is my thought that Religions which cannot evolve to teach love and mutual understanding, rather than fear and judgement, will eventually cease to exist.

Back to the core concept of spirit as energy. Everything is energy. Everything! All things physical and non-physical are energy in motion. Even thoughts, feelings, words, beliefs, emotions, actions, perceptions, and ways of moving through life all have a vibrational energy. Love-based energies have a higher vibration, and fear-based energies have a lower vibration. When you feel unrestricted, light, expansive, and enthusiastic, you are in the vibrations of love, and when you feel down, obstructed, pressured, repressed, and heavy, you are in fear. It truly is that simple.

When you become proficient at paying attention to how you feel, shifting from fear and darkness to love and light becomes easy and graceful; that is, for the most part. Life still throws circumstances your way, but you have the skills to navigate them with greater ease. And even when it isn't easy, you have the capacity to recognize what you are feeling and give it the loving attention being asked for.

New circumstances also require new perspectives. Looking through the eyes of love and understanding vs. through the eyes of fear and judgement can change everything.

Have you ever noticed how some people seem to suck the energy out of a room? Even if they physically appear to have it all together, energetically they are dark, gloomy, and filled with fear. Then there are others who seem to light up a room when they enter, regardless of their physical appearance. That is the power of love transmitting through them. They are literally conduits of love and light.

There are now numerous studies showing physical effects of love-based energies, as well as fear-based energies in everything from water and plants, to the human psyche and physical disease. I encourage you to do your own research and learn for yourself.

Your personal knowledge vs. believing whatever comes along, is very powerful. Just because someone has told you to believe something, doesn't make it true or true for you.

Spiritual truths can be found within the core of every religion. Those truths are loving, high-vibration, spiritual concepts which include faith, hope, trust, peace, etc., all of which are love-based. Our connection to these truths, which also exist within the core of every living being, are often difficult to access to their fullest potential through much religious dogma because of the fear-based beliefs that are built up around them, and the definition that religions have given them.

These fear-based beliefs are often sold as love-based, making it virtually impossible to decipher truth from deception, or to decipher fear from love. Much of humanity, in my perception, is stuck in this grey zone, unable to access the full love and light that exists within themselves. They cannot see and recognize that the way home to Love, AKA God, is through themselves, rather than through their belief systems.

Keeping humanity stuck in the mud, even if unintentional, ensures that we don't wander away and follow our own path. Fear creates a form of control seen as necessary to prevent chaos and maintain order. With love, the external control of fear is simply not necessary.

Fear of becoming a lost soul, and potentially losing those they love most, keeps many from leaving their religions, even when everything inside of them calls to take the road less traveled. Fear is the greatest controller of the fragile human mind. In genuine love, there is no cause for fear.

How can you know your truth? There is a simple and easily recognizable difference between personal truth and the universal truth. While universal truth is stable, constant, and unchanging, personal truth continues to grow and evolve as you grow. Your personal truth is the result of your own personal evolution, based on your unique perception of your many life experiences and what you learn from each of those experiences. This is what I often refer to as "the evolution of belief."

I believe that as we evolve individually and collectively, our own understanding of the nature of creation also evolves. In my own perception, the Universal Consciousness and Wisdom that many call God also continually evolves with every experience in the entire universe, as an infinite intelligence that never stops learning. Its universality expands as everything – all living things, on all planets, in all galaxies and universes – thinks, learns, grows, and experiences life. All of this becomes a part of the infinite universal consciousness.

Every belief, perception, thought, action, and experience is stored as a memory in the cloud drive of the universe. Everything in the Universe is continually learning, growing, expanding, evolving, and infinitely changing. In this awareness, creation and evolution are the same and we are the creators of our own evolution.

We are, each of us, always equally creating, simply through being. We are all of the same infinite value and we are all equally worthy of accessing the infinite creation, infinite love, and infinite understanding of all that is. Speaking for myself and others I know, many of us were taught by our religiosities that we must earn the right to love, earn the right to heaven, and earn the right to God's presence. In this belief, we are taught that we are not worthy of happiness until proven otherwise.

All of those are fear-based beliefs of a very conditionally loving God. For some of us, as I experienced in childhood, this God has a long list of conditions. These conditions were sold to us as unconditional love, leading to even greater fear and confusion about what love really is.

The Creative Intelligence of the universe that I have now come to know is vastly different from the God that I grew up with. In my view, all dogma is man-made and based on the concepts of the human mind in its limited capacity to comprehend the incomprehensible, as we strive in our attempts to understand what is beyond our intellectual grasp.

Because we live in a reality that is currently driven by fear, we are inclined to see all things through the eyes of fear, until we are able to learn to consciously see otherwise. Fear, in any form or context, creates the perception of separation from the ever-present energy of loving creation.

However, we have never been separate from the Source of all that is, except that our beliefs have made it so. It is always love-streaming through all of us at all times, and only we, by our own belief in separation, can halt the flow. Belief creates reality and the belief in separation creates the separation.

Just because you believe a thing to be true, or just because thousands, and perhaps millions or even billions of people believe something, doesn't mean it is true. There was a time when all known humanity believed the earth to be the center of the universe. Yet today we now have ample evidence that it simply isn't true. Beliefs create the perceived reality of current truth. Beliefs, held long enough, can even alter perceived realty. While a particular belief may be true for some, that doesn't mean it is true for all. Truth is always in the eye of the beholder – the one who holds it.

Finding your own truth requires that you be willing to step outside of yourself, look objectively at each of your beliefs, and determine if your belief is truly based in love or if there is any form of fear attached to it. Recognizing the truth is simple. If it feels based in fear, it's false, and if it feels based in love, it's true. Ultimately, knowing your truth is recognizing what it *feels* like for you.

Many people are involved in their churches for the sense of community they provide, more so than for the religious practice; many are there because of a sense of fear if they aren't involved. In this fear of judgement, they are often denying their own inner truth for the acceptance of those around them who often see through the filter of fear themselves. Pure, unconditional, unwavering love doesn't judge.

Unfortunately, the judgment, shunning, guilt, and shame, that is sometimes expressed through those whose minds are controlled by fear, often make it difficult for many individuals to feel safe being who they really are. How long each of us can continue pretending to be someone we know deep inside we are not, simply for the acceptance of those around us, is part of our personal acceptance of ourselves.

As we each give ourselves permission to be who we really are and find *our* true path, we give others permission to be their authentic selves as well. As we come to understand our own unique path, we give everyone the freedom to be who they came here to be and learn the lessons they came here to learn, free from the fear of external judgment.

We simply cannot judge another person's path as we learn to understand our own. We are all evolving on our own path of self-discovery, and that makes life truly extraordinary. When we live in our personal truth, consciously, beautifully, and lovingly, we give others the freedom to live in their truth, consciously, beautifully, and lovingly.

At some point, our truth and our purpose, the reason we are here, begin to supersede the fears and desires for others' acceptance. When that happens, we find the courage to take a quantum leap in our own personal evolution.

Every person has access to their truth. You can easily retrieve it by asking your soul/spirit to reveal *your* truth; however, you need to be ready to accept that many of the beliefs you thought were true are really the beliefs that others have placed upon you. You also need to be willing to accept that many of the beliefs that you have used throughout your life are beliefs that no longer serve you or your greatest good.

Every person's beliefs are the result of their own path, their unique perception of their life experiences, and their own soul's evolution through the cosmos (if that resonates with you). We are all on our own paths as we find our way home to the Love within ourselves. That path home to love and purpose is determined by our soul's evolution and the lessons each of our souls decide we want to learn in this lifetime. Just as there are seven-billion-plus people on the planet at this time, there are seven-billion-plus paths. Your path is yours and theirs is theirs. There is no one right way.

It is often difficult for many who have outgrown religion to keep from judging those who are still following a path within it. This judgement was one of my difficulties as I found my own way outside of religion, still carrying spite within me for my past and the pain that was caused by my parents' system of belief.

Part of my mid-life transition was learning not to judge those who choose to stay in religion, trusting what they know to be true for themselves. As I connected to my own resonance of Spirit more and more, I could begin to see all of it through the eyes of love and understanding. In this awareness I came to accept that it is simply their path and not mine.

It is not our place to judge anyone else's path or spew our non-dogma onto them. Forcing our way onto another makes us no better than those who attempt to force their religious beliefs onto us.

Instead, you can confidently be who you are and be a loving example of who you are, while letting them be who they need to be. Just like you, they are following their path and being the best person they know how to be. Although they may judge you, hold tight to the truth of who are and be the loving essence you were born to be.

It is important to recognize and understand that these words about religion and dogma are not meant to offend anyone who is religious. If you are presently associated with a particular belief system, please don't take these words personally. If your heart and soul are happy where you are, stay the course. You are exactly where your soul wants you to be. If it wanted you elsewhere, it would put you elsewhere.

The important thing is that you trust your own truth and path with love, rather than fear and judgement. If you are where you are because of fear, which often manifests itself as guilt, shame, judgement, and expectation, you may need to dig deeper and see if this is really where your soul wants you. If your beliefs cause you to radiate with love, light, and an open heart, you are on the right path.

Fear-based beliefs don't only come from religion, of course. For me, my beliefs stemmed from religion because it was all that I knew for most of my childhood. I wasn't ever exposed to anything else.

Fear-based beliefs can also be spread

through the air waves subconsciously, and sometimes they are spread intentionally, through family, friends, teachers, and so on. They can also come from print publications, television, the internet, and media. Some less obvious beliefs sit in the collective unconscious and we pick them up like frequencies through our minds. Some beliefs are old and ancient, so deeply hidden under centuries of beliefs layered on top of them that we don't even know of their existence until they are made evident. Whether we consciously know them or not, they still subtly affect the human experience.

Some of our subconscious personal beliefs are created by us as a way of making sense of our painful and often confusing experiences, particularly when are in early development as very young children.

Remember, this isn't about who is right and who is wrong. Everyone is doing the best they can with what they know and believing what they believe until a new belief comes along to replace the ones that no longer work. Some beliefs are simply more stubborn and persistent than others because they've been part of the human experience for so long. I call these hand-me-down beliefs.

Some people cling tight to their hand-me-downs as though they are a royal birthright and inheritance. Many hold on to their ancestors' beliefs as an antiquity that needs to be treasured. For some, their familial beliefs, like artifacts, are placed on a shelf, taken down and polished for special occasions, while other artifacts get used as part of a daily ritual. Some wear their hand-me-downs as designer labels, giving them a sense of belonging to an entitled group. And others cling to their inheritance as though their lives depend on it, and for them it just may.

Some hand-me-downs are so ancient they are now relics as we sit in awe of their artifacts behind glass in museums or make treks to ancient lands. Some are old, full of holes, and falling apart, while some are downright rotten.

For many of us, our hand-me-downs are worn out, have lost the luster they once had, and no longer fit the way we are told they need to.

Sometimes it's best to let old, broken things go as we clean up and release what no longer serves us personally or the greatest good for humanity. Those old, holy beliefs simply no longer work for many of us as we come to a new spiritual understanding that better fits our present and future journey into a more conscious and loving world.

Freeing your spirit begins with listening to your inner truth and questioning all your beliefs. Regardless of what those around you might have said when you were younger about what you need to believe and who you need to be, you are the only one who really knows what does and does not work for you. Regardless of whom may still be telling you what to do, you are the only person who knows what is really best for you. Ultimately, you are the only person who knows what is true for you.

As you free your spirit from the beliefs that have been placed upon you, and false beliefs you created as a way of making sense of the world, you will begin to understand more and more of what your soul already knows. This knowing often feels more like remembering rather than learning. Each "aha" moment feels like flashes of brilliance that you somehow already knew. You may not be able to explain how you know it, you just know.

Your soul is the always-loving aspect of you. It guides you in loving truth and empowers you to move forward. It will never put you down or make you feel small. That smallness is ego and false belief, misguiding you, holding you back and causing you to feel less-than. Your soul, your truth, will always lift you up and inspire you. It will take you to the ends of the universe if you know how to listen.

Our truth, as we begin to remember what our soul already knows, first sits with us as we remember who we are and why we are here. This process of raising our consciousness and our spiritual awareness begins to embody as us. The more we embody our higher truth, the more we are able to let go of and de-energize anything that is not higher awareness of truth. As we shift, our truth then spreads outward, into the world, simply by our being and living a new, higher vibration.

Our truth spreads into the world around us without having to say a word, and becomes part of the collective consciousness and truth. As we embody the loving truth, the entire world is changed. Understanding this, we can see that there really is no "singular" truth and we are all one in consciousness. Some simply remember, know and embody higher truth sooner and bring it forward for the masses to find within themselves.

Personal truth is simply what is true and best for you, understanding that you are a part of the whole truth, the universal loving truth of all that is. It is less about "your" truth and more about your understanding of Universal truth. Your understanding continues to evolve rather than be stuck in the absolutes of dogma.

"Don't be afraid to question. Questioning holds the secrets to the evolution of belief."

STEP 3:
QUESTION EVERYTHING

The greatest liberation for me was learning that it really was okay, even safe and empowering, to question. After spending all my childhood being told to never question anything, learning to question as an adult took a great deal of courage.

I was a pensive child and deeply wanted to understand. I have always been curious about spiritual concepts, even as a young girl. Somehow, I understood spiritual concepts my parents couldn't grasp and my thinking outside the box defied everything they believed. For them, the only way to explain my ideas were to label them as evil. After being punished for questioning on more than one occasion and convinced by adults around me that questioning was the devil trying to tempt me, I finally stopped asking questions.

I lost my nerve with every rejection and lost my voice of curiosity. But that did not stifle my curious mind. I've always had an analytical mind and just needed to feel safe pursuing my desire to know more. As I grew into adulthood, I had to learn that it was safe to be curious. It took time and patience to find my voice once again.

One of my favorite quotes – a mantra I now live by – is, "question everything."

In adulthood, while I grew in self-awareness and my desire to be free of fear-based beliefs, I began questioning everything I had once been led to believe. As my questioning expanded, the false beliefs began rising to the surface of my recollection for acknowledgment, processing, and transmutation. By processing my beliefs, those based in fear and deception started melting away and lost control over me.

The more I questioned my beliefs and unraveled those that no longer fit, the easier it became to recognize more of them. I still practice questioning my experiences and beliefs every day when something new comes up for resolution and understanding, and as more is placed into my field of understanding for greater analysis and discernment.

In this age when everyone is free to speak their truth, or at least their perception, out across the world in a matter of seconds over the internet, it has become all the more important to question everything. We've moved from the Information Age to the Age of Discernment, requiring each of us to develop the capacity to dig deeper into our own understanding and connect to a higher truth, in order to make sense of the bombardment of perspectives.

Discernment is a new muscle we are all learning to manage. We need to develop the discernment muscle to decipher between truth and deception. We need to be able to seek the truth in between the lines of agendas, paid for media propaganda, well-meaning storytellers, and rabbit-hole diggers – all of whom have their own spin on reality and perception of what we call real. We must be able to decipher between fear and falsehoods disguised as love and truth, and truth that can hurt to look at and reckon with, because of the fear driving beneath it.

We need to question what we are being told to think and believe. We need to decipher between those who transmit darkness and fear using loving language to suck us into their agenda. We need to recognize the truly loving individuals who unknowingly spread fear and hold them up in love until they can see.

The truth about fear is hidden in plain sight and deception is disguised as truth.

Fear disguised as love has always been one of humanity's downfalls. It is up to us, as workers in the Light, to question everything. We must be willing to look at the beliefs as ugly as they may be, to see if they are true, and as pretty as they may be, to recognize if they are false. We must be willing to question our own shadows and transmute them, and to do the same with our collective shadows as well. We cannot afford to take falsehoods into our new world.

In an age when anyone and everyone is free to speak their truth, or perception, we need, more than ever before, to question everything.

Questioning everything is extremely self-empowering and infinitely necessary. If we are to be spiritually free, we need to be willing to open our minds and hearts to new possibilities. When our minds are closed by forced, coerced, or panhandled beliefs, and our hearts have become encapsulated by fear, it becomes impossible to access and follow our own truth and make strong, steady choices.

Personal truth is in our core and is the reason we call it a *gut feeling*. This central core is our power center and science calls this the *second mind*. It can only be accessed with a free mind and a clear, softened heart.

While we've all heard the saying, "follow your heart," I find there is a conundrum with that quote. A human heart that is controlled and confined by fear cannot work to its full potential and is easily misguided and closed by a fearful mind. Fear causes the heart to harden and as such, we become paralyzed in our ability to recognize our true desires and decipher what is best for us because of the ego's need for security.

A mind controlled by fear and a hardened heart make it nearly impossible to reach deeper within ourselves into the loving truth found in our center.

Questioning stimulates the mind to open and begins to free the heart of its encapsulation. The human mind was created to be curious and to always question the past, analyze the present, and reach for future possibilities. It thrives in an environment where it can grow, stretch, expand, and push itself to become more than it already is. Curiosity stimulates creation.

Curiosity and questioning are part of what make us uniquely human. Questions are vital to the creation and evolution process. This desire for expansion and continual improvement is part of what many call the Divine Human Blueprint.

Unlike other species on our planet, which evolve out of necessity, human beings have the capacity to consciously evolve. This ability to consciously create and advance is how we are the likeness of what we call God. We are the creators of our reality, whether we like it or not. We are limitless inter-creators with each other. We create with everyone and everything on the entire planet at every given moment.

This inter-creation, much of which was once limited to small cultures over long periods of time, has now become entirely global and can be virtually immediate. Communication and co-creation are no longer limited to intricately connected groups, and what used to take years to create now takes only months, weeks, days, or even minutes to become a physical reality. What we have now is close to instant manifestation.

Perhaps it is time to really question how we are wielding this creative power. Everything each of us sees, speaks, does, feels, and touches can almost immediately affect all life on earth. Our freedom of choice requires that we use discernment now more than ever before, and it is vital that we understand the vast and great responsibility we have as inter-creators.

This continual questioning of the human

mind allows us to make tremendous advances in science, medicine, and technology. Hopefully, it will provide us with the ability to heal many of the problems our advances have created in our ignorance of how they would affect us and the planet in the long term. We are using cutting-edge tools with archaic beliefs. Questioning and evolving our beliefs will allow us to use our tools for creation and transformation, rather than weapons for destruction.

We are but children on an evolutionary scale, still learning how to play nicely with each other and take care of the place we all call home. As we learn and grow, hopefully we will take better care of each other and our planet, to move forward collectively into a more loving reality.

As with all children, we are compelled to ask questions and search for better answers.

Why, then, have we been so afraid to do this with our belief systems and dogmas? There was a time when torture and even death was the potential result for anyone daring to question those who deemed themselves divinely appointed, but not anymore. We live in a great time of freedom to think and speak our perspectives openly, notwithstanding that our openness may induce external judgement.

While everything in our world is in a quantum leap of evolution, our spiritual beliefs are evolving at a snail's pace. We have modern-day technology with ancient beliefs driving how we use our creations. We use them in fearfulness rather than in evolved consciousness. It is as though our belief systems are kicking and screaming like toddlers with a temper tantrum into the new century of enlightened thought. They seem to be outright fighting against the new reality based in love that many of us are trying to consciously co-create. In essence, they are blocking themselves from their own ascension.

What if we began asking new, deeper, more thoughtful questions? What if everything we have ever been taught about our human nature and the nature of that which we call God is wrong? What if we all stopped bickering over who is right and who is wrong? What if we really stopped fighting over how one path is better than another? What if we ended all hostility over, "what's yours is mine and what's mine is mine" like three-year-olds who are just trying to figure out how to get along? What if our belief systems stopped fighting over the right to claim human souls? What if we stopped arguing over who is loved more by Daddy in the sky? What if we finally, collectively outgrew our

Daddy issues? What if we brought Mommy along for the ride and started respecting Her?

What if we stopped using God's name in vain as justification for our petty differences? What if we stopped using God's name to warrant harm against each other and to validate human rights abuses? What if we stopped using God's name to rationalize our greed and wars? What if we stopped using God's name as reasoning for judgements against each other? What if we all stopped using God's name for our own vain purposes?

What if we had the decency to stop shunning those who have the courage to think outside the box and question their inherited beliefs? What if we gave others the space to really and fully believe as they choose (not to be confused with practice as they choose) and trust their own individual path? What if God really is unconditional love and everything else is a misconception created in the minds of men?

What if we asked questions and took the same approach to beliefs about our spiritual nature the same way we approach wanting a new understanding of our physical nature? Once upon a time, humans would be strung up, burned, drowned, tortured, or have their throats slit, or at the very least, get publicly humiliated for asking "what if?" What if we have now collectively grown up enough that it is safe to question our beliefs without the threat of terrorism to our minds, hearts, and bodies?

One of the best books I've found on this subject, as a confirmation of my own insights, is Neale Donald Walsch's book, *God's Message To The World: You've Got Me All Wrong*. If you are really open to rethinking everything you think you know about the nature of what we call God, it will cause you to do just that.

"Love is the infinite, ever present energy all things are made of."

STEP 4:
FEEL LOVE EVERYWHERE

Throughout my entire childhood, I was taught to believe in God as a humanoid male, a magical, mystical man who required me to get down on my knees and grovel if I wanted anything, and worship him just to prove that I deserved to be in His presence. He was an ego-driven, narcissistic father who loved his sons and created men in His image. Women, even his most chosen and pure daughters that he supposedly delighted in, were lowly servants of men – and that was all I would or could ever be.

After leaving home, I came to discover a whole new version of what many call God. This concept of God is far grander and infinitely more loving than the God made in the image and likeness of man. After a lifetime of believing in the God of man, and then no God at all, I came to see and fully grasp that God is love.

Many of our ancient texts teach that God is love, yet what does that really mean? This idea of God as love became overwritten with the concept that God is a male being, made in the very image and likeness of man. It made sense at the time, when it was all the human mind could comprehend.

If you, like me, were raised with the God of man, you may have a difficult time wrapping your mind around the concept of God as anything else other than an all-powerful man in the sky.

The idea that God is love, love has no gender, and God is simply, "I am that I am," may be nearly impossible to grasp. The thought that God is energy, existing and always present as all things, without specific form or human personality, may seem completely irrational in your mind, as it once was in mine. The concept that what we call God is Pure Energy, may seem unreasonable because we, much of humanity, believed in Him for so long.

The awareness that Infinite Intelligence and Infinite Wisdom are both simultaneously masculine and feminine, existing as pure loving energy, may seem impossible to imagine. This is because many people's imagination, along with their connection to inspiration, is limited to their present physical reality and beliefs they have held for so long; thus any other perception is incomprehensible. The idea that the many aspects of All That Is can exist purely without human function or emotion might be nearly unfathomable to grasp. It was for me, until I experienced for myself what love really is, and how the energy we call God, really is Love.

One morning several years ago, I stood alone in my kitchen washing dishes at the sink. Deep in the process of my own spiritual expansion, I had been sick with a flu virus and coughing for three weeks. Physically I felt fine, but the cough lingered long after the other symptoms left me. I sensed intuitively that my illness was more than just the flu. The impression my body gave me was that I was clearing a lifetime of old beliefs and literally coughing them out of my cellular makeup. I've since come to call it the Ascension Flu. It is really quite common during one's personal expansion.

That morning as I stood in the kitchen, I felt a flood of inexplicable energy move through me. It was pure bliss unlike anything I had ever experienced before, or have felt since, although I've often wished I could. It was a high beyond anything words can describe. I felt what I can only explain as absolute Love. Not the kind of love you feel when you make love with your partner or hold your children or any other kind of physical/emotional love. It was infinitely more than that. I felt a palpable energy of love as it surged into every cell of my being. I felt it in my veins, muscles, pores, and skin. It flooded out from my eyes, fingers, and toes. It was as if *I* were Love itself. That is when I realized what love really is. In that moment, I came to know that I am Love embodied as me.

After that moment, I began seeing and feeling love everywhere, the way Neo saw numbers in the *Matrix* movies. Love is the stuff that I am made of and is the very essence of everything I am. It is the life force that continually feeds my spirit, surges through my veins, and the energy that creates all things. It is the energy that sparks all life to life and grows all dreams. It exists in every blade of grass, the whisper of the wind, every grain of sand, the laughter of children, and every nucleus of every cell of everything that is and has ever been. It is the microcosm and macrocosm of all things. It is the binding agent that glues all beings together and bonds all things to form. It is the heaven within.

In that single exhilarating, life-altering moment in my kitchen, I understood what we call God really is Love...and love is all there is.

That is when I came to fully grasp that we have never been separate from it and can never be. In this limitless love, there is no judgement or expectation. There are no conditions. We don't have to earn its presence or try to impress it. Infinite Love is infinite. It never wavers, not even for a moment. Love doesn't judge, it doesn't need to be worshipped, we don't need to pay penance for it, beg for its forgiveness, or ask it for personal favors. It doesn't need to be bought or earned. It can't be packaged and sold. It has no wants, needs, or desires. It is always there, ever present, simply waiting for each of us to find it within ourselves and embolden it. All we need to do is turn within. There we have full access to the All power of Love.

The belief that we have to earn the right to an eternity of love or pay a price and suffer for it, is part of a grand illusion. Whether these fear-based theories were created intentionally as a means of controlling humanity or were simply a misunderstanding passed down through the centuries is inconsequential. Those beliefs were created at a time when humans were in their infancy and it was all those young human minds were capable of comprehending.

The idea that the creative force of the universe could exist as pure boundless energy was inconceivable; thus, we humans created Gods in our own image. First the many Gods, and then the One God.

The God of man was created in the image of man at a time when humanity believed all creation came from the seed of men and male animals, when it was believed that men were the creators of life and there was no concept of the womb and egg. It was believed that women existed to birth men's seed, nurture men's children, and build men's kingdoms, just as it was believed that all female animals existed to grow the male animal's offspring.

At the time it made perfect sense. That was their only concept of how life became life and there was no scientific evidence to show otherwise. They only knew what they saw in the fields, and what they saw became grounds for the practice of husbandry and polygamy. As men were perceived as the creators of all life, requiring virginal wombs to ensure their creations, it made sense that the God of all creation would also be a man. For some cultures, this led to the control and ownership of animals and women as assets to grow men's domain.

In these man-as-creator beliefs, various patriarchal systems of fear and control grew stronger and more virulent. As a result, we nearly severed our connection to the Divine Feminine and the Mother aspect of Source. In the throes of worshipping an angry, vengeful deity, made in the beingness, likeness, and personality of dominating men, we forgot about our Mother.

We left Her out of our collective story and our consciousness. In many of our beliefs, we belittled Her to nothing more than an unused womb. We left Her in Her garden as we went out into the world to battle our new awareness of right and wrong. We left Her daughters out of his-story and we ravaged Mother Earth. During the long reign of patriarchy, the Mother Creator and all things feminine were reduced to meeting the needs and desires of men. In many beliefs, The Divine Mother and Her daughters became servants of men. But through all that, She never left us and never stopped loving us.

As we now know, all of creation is both masculine and feminine, and both are equally necessary for the creation of all things. Now that we know better, we can believe better. Let us forgive our ancestors for not knowing what they could not have possibly known.

We are now at a time of rebalancing the masculine and feminine as all things feminine are being restored to their greatness and given the space to fully rise and shine. She, the Divine Feminine, Mother aspect of all that is, in all of Her glory and wisdom, is now being resurrected to take Her place at the mantle alongside the Divine Masculine many call God.

Many claim that we are now living in the time of the ascension and foretold resurrection. To those who are looking for specific signs, it may not look the way many of our religions imagined it would be. But evolution is not an event, it's a process. The return of Christ isn't about Jesus returning in grandiose physical form, and the resurrection isn't about zombies rising up from the dead. It is the return of Christ Consciousness, the consciousness of unconditional love; the resurrection is the upswelling of compassion and understanding, both of which arise from the restoration of Mother. Together, as one humanity, we are returning to Her peace and prosperity.

That love I felt in my kitchen was the Mother aspect of Source. It was Her compassion. It was Her, wanting me to feel Her loving arms around me, showing me what love really is. She is coming out of the depths to our planet's playground, manifesting Herself within each one of us to heal and nurture the broken hearts of Her children and restore peace to Her family.

She loves us no matter what – without condition or expectation. Even when we have treated Her, our home, and Earth's daughters with such indignity, She still loves us, and always has. Even when we collectively left Her in the Garden of Eden to follow the God of man, She never stopped watching over us, nurturing and supporting us. She loves all of us all equally and sees us all as magnificent. She wraps Her love around us with every breath of wind, wanting to heal our wounds, stop the boys from fighting, and clean up the mess we have made of our home and playground. Mother, as seen in the strong feminine presence now manifesting in our collective reality, is coming to the rescue. She is here to help us find our way home and as she does, the Divine Masculine, The Father aspect of God, can let down his defense and lead with love and protection, rather than anger and vengeance – a kinder, gentler masculine energy we no longer need to fear.

She, the Divine Feminine, is not asking us to replace the Masculine Father figure, only to stand in balance and equality with Him, at His side, not *from* His side. One misquote took us down a fearful and painful path, and now we are all coming home, back to Her garden and heaven on earth. We are remembering and re-becoming love, becoming who we always were.

When we fully understand that love is all there is, we are then able to see all things through the eyes of infinite love. We are able to see with unconditional love, the way God, by whatever name or label you give it, sees us. Through the eyes of love, we are able to see everything in ourselves and the world around us in complete acceptance and understanding. We can even love our enemies and those we believe spitefully use us to further their own agendas.

Human beings are remarkable creatures, capable of so much more than we realize. We have the capacity to create anything we imagine. We are even capable of creating the peace and heaven on earth we all say we want. We are so powerful that if enough of us really wanted it, heaven, here, could happen in an instant, not just for the lucky few, but for everyone.

If we can just understand that love never left us, we would never feel the need to fight over who deserves it and feel guilt over what it takes to earn it. We would have no desire to stray into greed and selfishness, which are based in fear, because we would already have all we need. We would have more than enough to give.

We are the ones who left the proverbial

garden of peace in our yearning for greater wisdom, and we are still trying to find our way home to it. Many belief systems teach about finding our way home to God and Heaven, without realizing that it has always been present within us.

Returning to love is simply a matter of understanding that we are all the essence of love. We are all one with love. We simply need to remember how to own it within ourselves.

If we can comprehend and accept that unconditional love in truth exists fully and completely without conditions or expectations, and learn to love ourselves unreservedly, the way that God/Source sees us, then everything in our world can easily change to follow suit. That is what it really means for us to love our neighbors and our enemies the way God loves us. As we begin diving within ourselves and see our own divinity, we can't help but see it in others and wish them well. We genuinely want them to be healed of their fearful disease because we know that their healed hearts become part of the higher collective consciousness. We understand that every person's consciousness is part of the whole. Rather than seeking revenge, we ask for their healing.

This is also what it means to love our neighbors as we love ourselves. All love begins with genuine self-love (not arrogance, which is based in fear). Everything that exists in our own personal periphery – every relationship, experience, perception, thought, belief, action, and choice – is a reflection of the relationship each of us has with ourselves.

When you are completely free to love all

of who you are, wholeheartedly, then you are free to love all of life and everyone in it. From there you can see that love, in all its grandeur, really is the most powerful force in the universe.

Love is so powerful it has the ability to transform and transmute all fear. Just as a room cannot stay dark when a light is switched on, fear cannot withstand the presence of love.

Those of us who see God as Love, rather than a magic man in the sky, feel an urge to use this understanding of the Allness of Love to help humanity to remember what love really is. We feel called and compelled to show what all people are capable of when each of us seeks to find the kingdom of heaven within ourselves.

In this understanding, we can see and experience the infinite, limitless possibilities found only in the power of love. It takes only

1% of the population, the other 1%, to shift the entire planetary experience out of fear and lack. That is how powerful love is.

The more we each recognize the power of love and accept ourselves as love embodied, the faster and easier it will be to create peace and heaven on Earth. We are the ground crew and it is up to us to create the world we desire.

This embodiment of love and being a loving, beneficial presence on the planet is more than just talking about love, peace, and harmony. Anyone can talk the talk. This is about walking the walk and being love in all things. It is embodying love in every thought, deed, word and action. It isn't about being perfect, it is simply catching ourselves when we are out of alignment with love and correcting our course. In the words of Jesus the Christ, (see John 10:34

and Psalm 82:6) we are all God. We are that we are, and love is that it is. We are all that. We just simply need to remember and be.

"Self-trust is the most difficult trust of all, and the most powerful."

STEP 5:

BE FREE TO TRUST

One of the harshest and most painful lessons I learned early in my childhood was to never trust anyone, especially myself. It came as the result of being hurt by those I was told I needed to trust most. Because I was taught to trust and obey my elders without question, even when they hurt me, I could no longer decipher who I could and couldn't trust. I found it safer to trust no one.

Misguided trust led to abuse. This abuse of trust by my superiors became the beginning of mistrusting the path my parents and religion told me that God had designed and predestined for me. As I grew, because of the pain that I felt inflicted upon me, I began to distrust my supposed predestined path as the path that was truly best for me. God's Plan, set forth by my parent's unique religion, began to feel contrived.

Because self-awareness and self-guidance was frowned upon as evil, I never knew to develop self-trust. The concepts of any self-awareness, or self-anything, were frowned upon. Real freedom of choice, my ability to make self-choices, did not come into my periphery until well into adulthood. In my early 20s, I stumbled across self-help books that fueled my desire to improve the conditions of my life and fed me the ability to look beyond my then-present mental restrictions. Those books began opening my mind and started me down my own path of changing everything I thought I knew. They challenged my previous assumptions and caused me to consider entirely new possibilities for my life, far beyond the fears ingrained in me during childhood.

Trust, however, was not within easy grasp. It was the most difficult of all awarenesses for me to wrangle with. Every person in my life I had wanted to trust, and was told I needed to trust, had hurt me. And because I had trusted them so freely, only to have them turn on me, I unconsciously developed the belief that I could not trust myself. That is, until I came to really see that I am the only one who always knows what's best for me. The only person in my life who hadn't hurt or abandoned me, was me.

Before I could come home to my own truth, I needed to learn how to discern what I had once believed and analyze all of the layers of beliefs that had been inflicted on me, which I had internalized and subsequently interpreted as my own beliefs. Many of those beliefs had been subconsciously playing me and directing my life through handed-down fear. Learning to trust myself and my own truth began with disbelieving what I had always believed. Challenging my existing ingrained beliefs and preconceptions was not easy, because disbelieving never is. Navigating and peeling off the many layers of fear-based beliefs and processing them with loving truths is incredibly liberating; it also requires a great deal of self-compassion.

Becoming free to trust your true self and the path that is best for you begins with rethinking everything you think you believe. I say it that way because beliefs are temporary and can be overwritten with new beliefs. Beliefs only control us as long as we think they do.

The perceptions of who we think we need to be, what we should do, what is expected from us, our beliefs in worthiness or worthlessness, begin for all of us when we are very young. As we grow, we each unconsciously buy into those external cues that are fed to us by others as truth, until their beliefs became embedded in our makeup and become what we assume to be our own truths.

Beliefs are different than truths in that beliefs are easily changed. We can change our paths, change our minds, and change what we believe; albeit change of this scope often takes time and diligence, because beliefs exist in layers, and each layer requires processing to varying degrees. The more we dig down through the layers of false beliefs, the more the truth begins to reveal itself. Truths are deeper than beliefs and evolve as a result of personal experience, change in consciousness, and deeper internal understanding. Truths feel different from beliefs as they come up from our center as an innate part of who we are.

Our beliefs are the result of concepts that were placed upon us as we grew or that we picked up throughout life based on external observations made by ourselves and others. Our beliefs came from our parents, siblings, religions, friends, teachers, and even the media. They were also created by us, often unconsciously as we moved through life as a way of making sense of our world and the world around us. Those fear-based beliefs that were created for us or placed on us as young children are the beliefs that have the greatest impact on our life and are often the most difficult to overwrite.

While our minds are still developing as young children, everything we see, hear, touch, learn, and experience is indelibly engrained in our minds until it becomes a part of who we see ourselves being. It is almost as if those beliefs become encoded in our DNA, and in a way they do. Those beliefs become particularly embedded and hard-wired into our being if there is drama or trauma attached with them.

This is part of the reason that fear is such an effective controlling device for many belief systems. Whether that fear and control is intentional or not, it is very effective. Fear of the consequences for questioning our beliefs, particularly when taught to the young, developing minds of children, keeps many from even considering another path, even if they are miserable on the path that has been supposedly chosen for them. Of course, this isn't to say that all religions are bad or that the fear-based indoctrination of young children is an intentional form of control. It is simply a pattern that has been replicated for hundreds, if not thousands, of years. It's a model that works to keep the business of religion alive and thriving, in the belief that those who manage them are doing what is best for followers. This was the model long before any human being understood psychology and the fragility of the human mind.

Now that we have a better understanding of psychology and the workings of the mind, we can begin rethinking and processing the beliefs that hold our spirits captive. Although many people think of psychology as a mental study, it was originally interlinked with spirituality. The word *psychology* literally translates to "study of the soul." The science of mind is actually a spiritual study. It just took me a long time to see and really understand their intricate and invaluable connection.

In 2008, I faced my mid-life crisis and the beginning of my mid-life rebirth. What I could not see at the beginning, as my life started falling apart, is that this was the breakdown that is part of the breakthrough. It was the falling-away that often occurs in any transformation. My life had to fall apart before I could become who I was really meant to be. In fact, what looked like my life falling apart was really my life coming together. As the pieces shattered, my old beliefs started surfacing for me to recognize, remedy, resolve, and process – that processing lead me to a much more beautiful version of myself and my life purpose.

Several years earlier, I had attended a writing retreat out of a desire to write my memoirs about growing up in a polygamist cult. Once piece of advice given at the retreat was to keep a notebook on hand at all times to jot down messages as my inner muse fed them to me. What I didn't expect were notes from my inner therapist. I had notebooks everywhere and as inspiration about how to fix my life came in, I wrote them down. As I wrote, my life seemed to come together, and for the first time in my life, I started to really love myself as a part of the process that my inner voice was teaching me.

One day I decided to input all of the notes from my various notebooks onto my computer for safekeeping, in a workable order. Those notes became the process in my first published book, *Transcending Fear*. It wasn't intentionally meant to be a book, just my own healing process; but it took on a life of its own and became a book that went on to change other people's lives as well as my own. It is a process anyone can use, regardless of where their beliefs came from.

When I wrote that first book, it became evident that the cause of my suffering was rooted in my childhood religion. I share how those fear-based beliefs from my childhood affected me as an adult and how I healed my life from the deep-seated effects that had been planted in my being. I came to see that much of the trauma I experienced as a child was the result of my parent's belief system, leaving me with a form of what I could only call P.T.S.D. (post-traumatic stress disorder). This resulted in my inability to use reasoning as a way to make self-supportive choices and prevented me from following my heart's desires.

Not long after publishing that first edition of *Transcending Fear*, Marlene Winell Ph.D., a professional psychologist, introduced a new diagnosis that fully explained why I had such a difficult time trusting myself and others. The definition of *Religious Trauma Syndrome* was spot-on for what I had experienced and felt after I ran away from home as a teenager. At that time, there were no professional services available, so I counseled myself with self-help books that literally saved my life. Now, however, there was evidence that my internal suffering was the result of my parent's dogma.

The official term for what I had experienced was simply a confirmation of what I already knew and the healing process I had already experienced. In my 20s, through my own self-therapy, I learned the concept of self-responsibility, which literally saved my life. Self-trust, however, was still a concept that I could not wrap my head around. I looked at my life and saw so many poor decisions as a result of never being taught as a child how to make decisions.

My childhood religion taught that the whole purpose for life was free-will-choice. But then I was told to never make any wrong choices, never make any choices that weren't pre-approved by the men in charge, and to never make mistakes. That way, someday when I died, if I had been good enough and followed all their right rules, then I could go to heaven. In my case, as a female, my future husband determined if I was worthy to go to heaven and he got to decide whether to let me in or not. I sometimes joke that my religion was Patriarchy on steroids.

For me, I found it was safest to never choose at all. Hence, I knew nothing about how to make choices or how to remedy situations as they arose. Instead, all my mistakes and inability to protect myself led to self-loathing. Running away from home was the first real choice I had ever made for myself – a choice made purely out of desperation, with no concept of consequences.

In early adulthood, self-help books began teaching me that my choices directed my life; it was not predestined by anyone else. Knowing that I no longer had to live by default gave me a new outlook on life. It took away the fear, shame, and guilt that had followed me with the label of being an apostate.

Unfortunately, making decisions was a painful process that took me years to learn and I sometimes still struggle with it. That is, until I remember to stop listening to the beliefs in my mind and trust the truth in my core. It always comes down to looking deep inside to recognize beliefs that may be out of alignment. When I remember to follow the process of my own inner guidance, rather than being distracted by other people's beliefs, everything realigns.

It always returns to self-trust, listening to my own inner truth, and being willing to dig deep down into my thoughts and beliefs to find those that hold my spirit – and my ease – captive. When I quiet the chatter in my mind and become still, my inner voice guides me with clarity.

Rethinking everything you have come to subconsciously believe doesn't mean you have to change all your beliefs; it does, however, require the willingness to dig down through the layers upon layers of beliefs and determine which do and do not ring true for you. As beliefs come to the surface to be remedied, your truths may begin to change as you spiritually evolve to new understanding, and as a new level of truth is revealed.

This process is essentially like digging for coal and turning the coal into diamonds. The best gems of life can be found in the darkest places. Being spiritually free requires that you have the fortitude and courage to dig into the dimmest recesses of your mind, the darkest stories of your past, and the most painful memories of your lifetime and even beyond. It requires the recognition that not only are many of your beliefs no longer serving you, but often they are in complete opposition to your truth. Your beliefs, in fact, may actually be preventing you from achieving your highest potential.

False beliefs may be blocking you from your own greatest good and being of maximum service to yourself and humanity; they limit you from the fullness of who you are here to be. You can easily decipher if beliefs are false and fear-based by the way they feel. The truth, the voice you can trust, is always loving.

Your beliefs reside in your mind and are often attached to ego. They sit at the surface and continually filter into every aspect of your life, even throughout your physical body, causing you to feel out of ease. Many beliefs, when out of alignment with truth, result in physical disease.

When your beliefs are held within loving consciousness and aligned with your core truth, the mind becomes a lead generator, searching for resources that align with what your truth is telling you. From this place of alignment, your mind becomes limitlessly resourceful.

Your heart is a built-in force that pulls you toward the life you desire; not what you think you want, but what resonates with the light in your heart. When your heart is ignited by your loving truth, it lights up every room and life it touches. It becomes unstoppable in its desire to shift your life experiences and the world around you.

The truth of who you are is in your core: the life force that sparks your enthusiasm and enables your way. It powers the heart with truth and propels you forward. Deep inside, that gut feeling you may feel at times, and even that fire in your belly that drives you, is your truth.

Your spirit is the energy that you carry in, through, and around yourself. It can often be seen or felt extending out from you as your aura.

The lighter your energy, the more peaceful and powerful it is. When you learn to align all four aspects of your being – mind, heart, body, and spirit – then life flows almost as if by magic.

Once there, you can hold yourself high, high-minded in the highest consciousness of love. Here, in the loving, everything you think, speak, feel, and do is out of love for the whole human race and for all life on earth. Here there is no division, no "us vs. them," no winners and losers, no right or wrong way. Here there is only understanding that we are all love as energy, having a human experience. Here your spirit is free to be all that you can imagine and to lift others up to do the same.

Getting to that point begins with examining the surface beliefs in your mind. You've most likely heard the saying, "it's all in your head"…and in a way, it is.

As your mind opens to new possibilities and you begin to question your beliefs, the fear that had once encapsulated your heart starts to melt away, giving you more access to your truth. When you align the truth in your core, the desire in your now-open heart, and new empowering beliefs in your mind with the energy of genuine love, anything becomes possible. At the least, you can experience life in new, more empowering ways than you may have ever imagined possible.

When the mind, body, heart, and spirit are all aligned in loving, the journey of life feels at ease and heaven really is within.

My best advice for freeing your spirit and learning to trust is to listen to yourself rather than the "shoulds" of anyone else. Clear your mind, clear your heart, clear your energy field, and just ask yourself, "what's best?" The answer will come. You can sense it and it always feels exactly right. Some may call this a form of prayer; I call it tuning in to my own inner guidance. It is always spot on if I listen and act on what I hear inside.

When you learn to listen to your deepest inner guidance you will find that, regardless of life's circumstances, you can always trust yourself.

"Peace is a process and not a destination. Be patient with yourself as you work toward making peace."

Conclusion

Freeing your spirit is so much more than spiritual freedom, and certainly more than freedom from religion. It is freedom to be wholly and souly true to oneself in mind, body, heart, and spirit. It is the freedom from fear of expectation and from the fragmentation that occurs as a result of allowing others' beliefs and perceptions to control your own self-liberty.

This is where your own personal magic happens and life begins to unfold in beautiful, unimaginable ways. As you free yourself to be less of who you've always been told you need to be – by others, society, and even yourself – you become who you were always meant to be. This releasing of past beliefs and perceptions may not always be easy; it may even hurt, as processing can be painful. But the end result is that you become fearlessly free to be who your soul designed you to be.

This, Dear One, is the quest each person faces in their human experience, whether they realize it or not. It is the quest to come home to yourself, as yourself, and remember the loving essence that you are, embodied as you. Many religions have taught that the quest is to die and return to God, with some form of judgment or expectation required to make that full return. That is a misperception, created in the minds of men and designed after the egos of men.

God is Love. Our real quest, the purpose for human existence, is to find love within ourselves and to be an expression of that love. It is to prove that through the fear and darkness, through the constructs of chaos, we can return home to the truth and love in ourselves.

Each one of us is the light and the way. Each one of us is divine light, streaming through us as pure bliss wanting to express itself as us. Each one of us is Divine Love, embodied in human form, wanting to express itself as the extraordinarily unique and special beings we all are. As we come to know and embody that we are emanations of love and light, we can then see that the only way to God is through ourselves, because we are all the embodiment of God. If God is Love and God is everywhere present, then we are also all one with God.

This is what the Christ attempted to teach before his words were interpreted to meet the controls of men and their religions in his name. He came to teach spiritual freedom, to teach his people how to free their spirits from the limitation and beliefs that they must go through religion to get to God. He came to teach that sacrifice was not necessary to appease God and that no one need pay money or penance for the right to God's presence.

This concept of Jesus as a spiritual master and God as the energy of Love, was once nearly impossible for my mind to grasp. The dogma of my childhood had such a grip on my mind, body, heart, and spirit that all I knew was suffering in life to prove myself worthy of an afterlife in a heaven created for men to become Gods. As I began to get free from the constraints of religion and open my mind to new possibilities, higher understanding began to flow through me. This new understanding is so much more beautiful, peaceful, loving, and spiritual than anything found in any of the beliefs of my childhood.

As divine love began flowing more freely through me, I could see how fear had been sold to me as love and used as a means of control, not only in my own religion, but in others as well.

The truth of divine love and the secrets of the universe are hidden within every religion, disguised within the framework of fear. Within this fear-based framework, a deep, rich, and long-lasting connection to spirit is difficult to maintain. This is why the human heart and spirit returns to church every week and needs to be fed again as life gets in the way; the spirit, under the confines of fear, needs a weekly boost. The spiritual high cannot last long under the umbrella of fear. As the high dissipates, fear sets back in and we need another spiritual dose to raise the high.

What if regular dosing wasn't necessary? What if you could stay in that high, most of the time, without a continual infusion of religion or relying on medication to keep you above the fray? What if you could stay out of fear and in love most, if not all, of the time? That is spiritual freedom. It is the ability to maintain the loving state within yourself and continue to reach for higher ground. All of that is available to you anytime and anywhere, as you begin to recognize and discern whether your beliefs and self-talk are based in fear or based in love.

Fear creates the illusion that you are separate from love. But love is who we all are, and the love you attract into your life is only your love being reflected back to you. The big love, Divine Love, love that feeds and infuses joy into all things, is always with you. It is simply up to you to magnify it forward.

Freeing your spirit from the constraints of fear-based beliefs gives you the capacity to follow and trust the path your soul is leading you on. If there are those in your life who are trying to guilt and shame you for the path you are taking, or shunning you for leaving your religion to follow a more spiritually-guided direction, take the higher road and love them where they are. They are judging you and your path out of their own fear. They are afraid for you because they care about you. Remember, caring and compassion are the core nature of human beings, rather than the competition and combativeness we've been sold. Trusting your own path is triggering a fear in them that only they can resolve within themselves. You choose love and compassion on your path to freedom from fear. Courage to you as you move forward. Trust who you are here to be and always hold yourself high as an example of what's possible when one chooses Love and Light over fear and darkness.

That Divine Love, moving through you as you, cancels out fear and makes it possible to face the seemingly impossible. In Love, you trust the path that calls to you, that desire to be of service and help make the world a better place. That trust is greater than any perception of fear. With Love, all things are possible!

ABOUT THE AUTHOR

Victoria Reynolds is a Spiritual Luminary and global Light Leader. The focus of her personal work is helping humanity find freedom from fear-based beliefs.

Through her inspirational writing, public presentations, personal guidance sessions and home-study programs, she helps individuals uncover their deepest fear-based beliefs, fuel their soul's unique purpose, expand their consciousness, and heal their past pain story.

Victoria emphasizes that her greatest

achievement to date is learning how to love all of life despite its many imperfections.

To learn more and to stay connected, visit her website at VictoriaReynolds.com.

FREE YOUR SPIRIT NOTES

FREE YOUR SPIRIT NOTES

FREE YOUR SPIRIT NOTES

www.ingramcontent.com/pod-product-compliance
Lightning Source LLC
Chambersburg PA
CBHW051843090426
42736CB00011B/1930